Christian Marriage Counseling Book of Bible Verses

Marriage Scriptures to help Women, Men, Kids, Moms & Couples with Intimacy, Sex & Communication

By Brian Mahoney

TABLE OF CONTENTS

INTRODUCTION:
Rightly Dividing the Truth

Part 1:
Scriptures for Selecting a Partner

Part 2:
Scriptures on the Benefits of Marriage

Part 3:
Scriptures on Love Respect & Forgive One Another

Part 4:
Scriptures with Instructions for Men

Part 5:
Scriptures with Instructions for Women

Part 6:
Scriptures on Sexual Relations

Part 7:
Scriptures on Marriage, Divorce & Remarriage

CONCLUSION
The Whole Armour of God

Copyright © 2021 MahoneyProducts
All rights reserved.

DEDICATION

**This book is dedicated to my Father
Ulester Mahoney Sr.**

ACKNOWLEDGMENTS

I WOULD LIKE TO ACKNOWLEDGE ALL THE HARD WORK OF THE MEN AND WOMEN OF THE UNITED STATES MILITARY, WHO RISK THEIR LIVES ON A DAILY BASIS, TO MAKE THE WORLD A SAFER PLACE.

INTRODUCTION

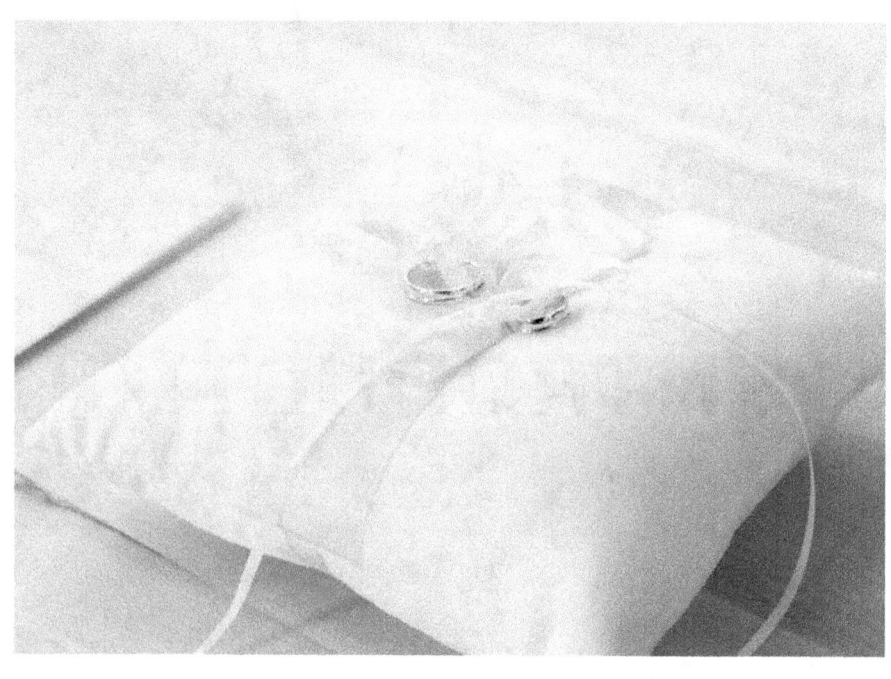

RIGHTLY DIVIDING THE TRUTH

Before you begin with scriptures and bible verses about **marriage**, I would like to briefly cover the importance of understanding.

Matthew 7:21-27 (KJV)

21 Not every one that saith unto me, Lord, Lord, shall enter into the kingdom of heaven; but he that doeth the will of my Father which is in heaven.

22 Many will say to me in that day, Lord, Lord, have we not prophesied in thy name? and in thy name have cast out devils? and in thy name done many wonderful works?

23 And then will I profess unto them, I never knew you: depart from me, ye that work iniquity.

24 Therefore whosoever heareth these sayings of mine, and doeth them, I will liken him unto a wise man, which built his house upon a rock:

25 And the rain descended, and the floods came, and the winds blew, and beat upon that house; and it fell not: for it was founded upon a rock.

26 And every one that heareth these sayings of mine, and doeth them not, shall be likened unto a foolish man, which built his house upon the sand:

27 And the rain descended, and the floods came, and the winds blew, and beat upon that house; and it fell: and great was the fall of it.

Matthew 7:21-27 shows us the danger of wrongly dividing the truth. How sad to see a person who believes that Jesus is Lord and is doing what he believes is many wonderful works in the name of the Lord, only to hear, in the day of judgement "depart from me".

2 Timothy 2:15 (KJV)

Study to shew thyself approved unto God, a workman that needeth not to be ashamed, rightly dividing the word of truth.

We must rightly divide the truth. 2 Timothy 2:15 tells us that the solution to understanding bible truth is not just to read the Bible but to study it. Here is just 1 of many strategies you can use improve our understanding of the bible, and rightly divide the truth.

Read the Bible frequently

Acts 17:11 (KJV)

These were more noble than those in Thessalonica, in that they received the word with all readiness of mind, and searched the scriptures daily, whether those things were so.

This verse from Acts 17 tells us, they searched the scriptures daily. Sometimes all's it takes is just one scripture in the morning to put you in the proper frame of mind for the entire day!

Joshua 1:7-8 (KJV)

7 Only be thou strong and very courageous, that thou mayest observe to do according to all the law, which Moses my servant commanded thee: turn not from it to the right hand or to the left, that thou mayest prosper withersoever thou goest

8 This book of the law shall not depart out of thy mouth; but thou shalt meditate therein day and night, that thou mayest observe to do according to all that is written therein: for then thou shalt make thy way prosperous, and then thou shalt have good success.

Later on in the book of Joshua we learn that someone did turn either right or left from the word. Not only did it cost that person and their family their life, the entire congregation suffered.

Notice that the scriptures use the words "daily" and "day and night" to emphasize the frequency needed for understanding.

It is nice to attend bible classes and hear sermons, but you have to search the scriptures for yourself to help in maximizing your understanding.

Psalm 119:10-12

10 With my whole heart have I sought thee: O let me not wander from thy commandments.

11 Thy word have I hid in mine heart, that I might not sin against thee.

12 Blessed art thou, O Lord: teach me thy statutes.

The Bible heart is your mind. In biblical terminology, statutes (Hebrew choq) refers to laws given without any reason or justification.

Hebrews 11:1 Now faith is the substance of things hoped for, the evidence of things not seen.

Offen times following these laws will require a great deal of faith.

Hebrews 11:6 But without faith it is impossible to please him: for he that cometh to God must believe that he is, and that he is a rewarder of them that diligently seek him.

Congradulations on seeking the commandments and laws of God.

2 Timothy 3:16-17 King James Version

16 All scripture is given by inspiration of God, and is profitable for doctrine, for reproof, for correction, for instruction in righteousness:

17 That the man of God may be perfect, thoroughly furnished unto all good works.

Now let's see what God has to say about....**marriage**

BIBLE VERSES AND SCRIPTURES ABOUT MARRIAGE

PART 1

Selecting a Partner

PHYSICAL ATTRACTION

Song of Solomon 4:9   KJV

9 Thou hast ravished my heart, my sister, my spouse; thou hast ravished my heart with one of thine eyes, with one chain of thy neck.

LIKE MINDED SPIRITUALLY

1 Corinthians 9:5   KJV

5 Have we not power to lead about a sister, a wife, as well as other apostles, and as the brethren of the Lord, and Cephas?

2 Corinthians 6:14-18   KJV

14 Be ye not unequally yoked together with unbelievers: for what fellowship hath righteousness with unrighteousness? and what communion hath light with darkness?

15 And what concord hath Christ with Belial? or what part hath he that believeth with an infidel?

16 And what agreement hath the temple of God with idols? for ye are the temple of the living God; as God hath said, I will dwell in them, and walk in them; and I will be their God, and they shall be my people.

17 Wherefore come out from among them, and be ye separate, saith the Lord, and touch not the unclean thing; and I will receive you.

18 And will be a Father unto you, and ye shall be my sons and daughters, saith the Lord Almighty.

GOOD MARRIAGE TRAITS

Proverbs 20:6-7　　　　　**KJV**

6 Most men will proclaim every one his own goodness: but a faithful man who can find?

7 The just man walketh in his integrity: his children are blessed after him.!

Psalm 37:16　　　　　**KJV**

16 A little that a righteous man hath is better than the riches of many wicked.

Amos 3:3　　　　　**KJV**

3 Can two walk together, except they be agreed?

Colossians 3:12-13

12 Put on therefore, as the elect of God, holy and beloved, bowels of mercies, kindness, humbleness of mind, meekness, longsuffering;

13 Forbearing one another, and forgiving one another, if any man have a quarrel against any: even as Christ forgave you, so also do ye.

AVOID THESE TRAITS

1 Timothy 5:8   **KJV**

But if any provide not for his own, and specially for those of his own house, he hath denied the faith, and is worse than an infidel.

Proverbs 21:9   **KJV**

9 It is better to dwell in a corner of the housetop, than with a brawling woman in a wide house.

Proverbs 21:19   **KJV**

19 It is better to dwell in the wilderness, than with a contentious and an angry woman.

Proverbs 12:4   **KJV**

4 A virtuous woman is a crown to her husband: but she that maketh ashamed is as rottenness in his bones.

Proverbs 22:24-25   **KJV**

24 Make no friendship with an angry man; and with a furious man thou shalt not go:

25 Lest thou learn his ways, and get a snare to thy soul.

PART 2

Benefits of Marriage

Ecclesiastes 4:9-12   KJV

9 Two are better than one; because they have a good reward for their labour.

10 For if they fall, the one will lift up his fellow: but woe to him that is alone when he falleth; for he hath not another to help him up.

11 Again, if two lie together, then they have heat: but how can one be warm alone?

12 And if one prevail against him, two shall withstand him; and a threefold cord is not quickly broken.

Ecclesiastes 9:9   KJV

9 Live joyfully with the wife whom thou lovest all the days of the life of thy vanity, which he hath given thee under the sun, all the days of thy vanity: for that is thy portion in this life, and in thy labour which thou takest under the sun.

Proverbs 18:22   KJV

22 Whoso findeth a wife findeth a good thing, and obtaineth favour of the Lord.

Genesis 2:18   KJV

18 And the Lord God said, It is not good that the man should be alone; I will make him an help meet for him.

Proverbs 31:10 **KJV**

10 Who can find a virtuous woman? for her price is far above rubies.

11 The heart of her husband doth safely trust in her, so that he shall have no need of spoil.

12 She will do him good and not evil all the days of her life.

13 She seeketh wool, and flax, and worketh willingly with her hands.

14 She is like the merchants' ships; she bringeth her food from afar.

15 She riseth also while it is yet night, and giveth meat to her household, and a portion to her maidens.

16 She considereth a field, and buyeth it: with the fruit of her hands she planteth a vineyard.

17 She girdeth her loins with strength, and strengtheneth her arms.

18 She perceiveth that her merchandise is good: her candle goeth not out by night.

19 She layeth her hands to the spindle, and her hands hold the distaff.

20 She stretcheth out her hand to the poor; yea, she reacheth forth her hands to the needy.

21 She is not afraid of the snow for her household: for all her household are clothed with scarlet.

22 She maketh herself coverings of tapestry; her clothing is silk and purple.

23 Her husband is known in the gates, when he sitteth among the elders of the land.

24 She maketh fine linen, and selleth it; and delivereth girdles unto the merchant.

25 Strength and honour are her clothing; and she shall rejoice in time to come.

26 She openeth her mouth with wisdom; and in her tongue is the law of kindness.

27 She looketh well to the ways of her household, and eateth not the bread of idleness.

28 Her children arise up, and call her blessed; her husband also, and he praiseth her.

29 Many daughters have done virtuously, but thou excellest them all.

30 Favour is deceitful, and beauty is vain: but a woman that feareth the Lord, she shall be praised.

PART 3

Love, respect and forgive one another

Psalm 85:10   KJV

10 Mercy and truth are met together; righteousness and peace have kissed each other.

Ephesians 4:2-3   KJV

2 With all lowliness and meekness, with longsuffering, forbearing one another in love;

3 Endeavouring to keep the unity of the Spirit in the bond of peace.

Ephesians 4:32   KJV

32 And be ye kind one to another, tenderhearted, forgiving one another, even as God for Christ's sake hath forgiven you.

1 John 4:7   KJV

7 Beloved, let us love one another: for love is of God; and every one that loveth is born of God, and knoweth God.

Colossians 3:14   KJV

14 And above all these things put on charity, which is the bond of perfectness.

1 Peter 4:8   KJV

8 And above all things have fervent charity among yourselves: for charity shall cover the multitude of sins.

1 Corinthians 16:14 KJV

14 Let all your things be done with charity.

1 Corinthians 11:9-12   KJV

9 Neither was the man created for the woman; but the woman for the man.

10 For this cause ought the woman to have power on her head because of the angels.

11 Nevertheless neither is the man without the woman, neither the woman without the man, in the Lord.

12 For as the woman is of the man, even so is the man also by the woman; but all things of God.

1 Corinthians 13:1-13   KJV

Though I speak with the tongues of men and of angels, and have not charity, I am become as sounding brass, or a tinkling cymbal.

2 And though I have the gift of prophecy, and understand all mysteries, and all knowledge; and though I have all faith, so that I could remove mountains, and have not charity, I am nothing.

3 And though I bestow all my goods to feed the poor, and though I give my body to be burned, and have not charity, it profiteth me nothing.

4 Charity suffereth long, and is kind; charity envieth not; charity vaunteth not itself, is not puffed up,

5 Doth not behave itself unseemly, seeketh not her own, is not easily provoked, thinketh no evil;

6 Rejoiceth not in iniquity, but rejoiceth in the truth;

7 Beareth all things, believeth all things, hopeth all things, endureth all things.

8 Charity never faileth: but whether there be prophecies, they shall fail; whether there be tongues, they shall cease; whether there be knowledge, it shall vanish away.

9 For we know in part, and we prophesy in part.

10 But when that which is perfect is come, then that which is in part shall be done away.

11 When I was a child, I spake as a child, I understood as a child, I thought as a child: but when I became a man, I put away childish things.

12 For now we see through a glass, darkly; but then face to face: now I know in part; but then shall I know even as also I am known.

13 And now abideth faith, hope, charity, these three; but the greatest of these is charity.

PART 4

Instructions for Men

Genesis 2:20-24   KJV

20 And Adam gave names to all cattle, and to the fowl of the air, and to every beast of the field; but for Adam there was not found an help meet for him.

21 And the Lord God caused a deep sleep to fall upon Adam, and he slept: and he took one of his ribs, and closed up the flesh instead thereof;

22 And the rib, which the Lord God had taken from man, made he a woman, and brought her unto the man.

23 And Adam said, This is now bone of my bones, and flesh of my flesh: she shall be called Woman, because she was taken out of Man.

24 Therefore shall a man leave his father and his mother, and shall cleave unto his wife: and they shall be one flesh.

Deuteronomy 24:5   KJV

5 When a man hath taken a new wife, he shall not go out to war, neither shall he be charged with any business: but he shall be free at home one year, and shall cheer up his wife which he hath taken.

Malachi 2:13-16   KJV

13 And this have ye done again, covering the altar of the Lord with tears, with weeping, and with crying out, insomuch that he regardeth not the offering any more, or receiveth it with good will at your hand.

14 Yet ye say, Wherefore? Because the Lord hath been witness between thee and the wife of thy youth, against whom thou hast dealt treacherously: yet is she thy companion, and the wife of thy covenant.

15 And did not he make one? Yet had he the residue of the spirit. And wherefore one? That he might seek a godly seed. Therefore take heed to your spirit, and let none deal treacherously against the wife of his youth.

16 For the Lord, the God of Israel, saith that he hateth putting away: for one covereth violence with his garment, saith the Lord of hosts: therefore take heed to your spirit, that ye deal not treacherously.

1 Corinthians 11:3   KJV

3 But I would have you know, that the head of every man is Christ; and the head of the woman is the man; and the head of Christ is God.

Colossians 3:19   **KJV**

19 Husbands, love your wives, and be not bitter against them.

1 Timothy 3:2   **KJV**

2 A bishop then must be blameless, the husband of one wife, vigilant, sober, of good behaviour, given to hospitality, apt to teach;

1 Timothy 3:12   **KJV**

12 Let the deacons be the husbands of one wife, ruling their children and their own houses well.

1 Peter 3:7   **KJV**

7 Likewise, ye husbands, dwell with them according to knowledge, giving honour unto the wife, as unto the weaker vessel, and as being heirs together of the grace of life; that your prayers be not hindered.

Colossians 3:19

19 Husbands, love your wives, and be not bitter against them.

Ephesians 5:25-33   **KJV**

25 Husbands, love your wives, even as Christ also loved the church, and gave himself for it;

26 That he might sanctify and cleanse it with the washing of water by the word,

27 That he might present it to himself a glorious church, not having spot, or wrinkle, or any such thing; but that it should be holy and without blemish.

28 So ought men to love their wives as their own bodies. He that loveth his wife loveth himself.

29 For no man ever yet hated his own flesh; but nourisheth and cherisheth it, even as the Lord the church:

30 For we are members of his body, of his flesh, and of his bones.

31 For this cause shall a man leave his father and mother, and shall be joined unto his wife, and they two shall be one flesh.

32 This is a great mystery: but I speak concerning Christ and the church.

33 Nevertheless let every one of you in particular so love his wife even as himself; and the wife see that she reverence her husband.

PART 5

Instructions for women

1 Corinthians 11:3   KJV

3 But I would have you know, that the head of every man is Christ; and the head of the woman is the man; and the head of Christ is God.

Colossians 3:18   KJV

18 Wives, submit yourselves unto your own husbands, as it is fit in the Lord.

1 Timothy 5:14   KJV

14 I will therefore that the younger women marry, bear children, guide the house, give none occasion to the adversary to speak reproachfully.

1 Peter 3:1-5   KJV

Likewise, ye wives, be in subjection to your own husbands; that, if any obey not the word, they also may without the word be won by the conversation of the wives;

2 While they behold your chaste conversation coupled with fear.

3 Whose adorning let it not be that outward adorning of plaiting the hair, and of wearing of gold, or of putting on of apparel;

4 But let it be the hidden man of the heart, in that which is not corruptible, even the ornament of a meek and quiet spirit, which is in the sight of God of great price.

5 For after this manner in the old time the holy women also, who trusted in God, adorned themselves, being in subjection unto their own husbands:

Ephesians 5:22-24   **KJV**

22 Wives, submit yourselves unto your own husbands, as unto the Lord.

23 For the husband is the head of the wife, even as Christ is the head of the church: and he is the saviour of the body.

24 Therefore as the church is subject unto Christ, so let the wives be to their own husbands in every thing.

Proverbs 19:14   **KJV**

14 House and riches are the inheritance of fathers: and a prudent wife is from the Lord.

Titus 2:4-5   **KJV**

4 That they may teach the young women to be sober, to love their husbands, to love their children,

5 To be discreet, chaste, keepers at home, good, obedient to their own husbands, that the word of God be not blasphemed.

1 Thessalonians 4:3   **KJV**

3 For this is the will of God, even your sanctification, that ye should abstain from fornication:

Genesis 3:16   **KJV**

16 Unto the woman he said, I will greatly multiply thy sorrow and thy conception; in sorrow thou shalt bring forth children; and thy desire shall be to thy husband, and he shall rule over thee.

1 Timothy 3:11   **KJV**

11 Even so must their wives be grave, not slanderers, sober, faithful in all things.

Proverbs 22:6   **KJV**

6 Train up a child in the way he should go: and when he is old, he will not depart from it.

Romans 12:2   **KJV**

And be not conformed to this world: but be ye transformed by the renewing of your mind, that ye may prove what is that good, and acceptable, and perfect, will of God.

Ephesians 6:10   **KJV**

10 Finally, my brethren, be strong in the Lord, and in the power of his might.

PART 6

Sexual Relations

Genesis 1:27-28 KJV

27 So God created man in his own image, in the image of God created he him; male and female created he them.

28 And God blessed them, and God said unto them, Be fruitful, and multiply, and replenish the earth, and subdue it: and have dominion over the fish of the sea, and over the fowl of the air, and over every living thing that moveth upon the earth.

Proverbs 5:18-19 KJV

18 Let thy fountain be blessed: and rejoice with the wife of thy youth.

19 Let her be as the loving hind and pleasant roe; let her breasts satisfy thee at all times; and be thou ravished always with her love.

Hebrews 13:4 KJV

4 Marriage is honourable in all, and the bed undefiled: but whoremongers and adulterers God will judge.

1 Corinthians 7:1-9 KJV

Now concerning the things whereof ye wrote unto me: It is good for a man not to touch a woman.

2 Nevertheless, to avoid fornication, let every man have his own wife, and let every woman have her own husband.

3 Let the husband render unto the wife due benevolence: and likewise also the wife unto the husband.

4 The wife hath not power of her own body, but the husband: and likewise also the husband hath not power of his own body, but the wife.

5 Defraud ye not one the other, except it be with consent for a time, that ye may give yourselves to fasting and prayer; and come together again, that Satan tempt you not for your incontinency.

6 But I speak this by permission, and not of commandment.

7 For I would that all men were even as I myself. But every man hath his proper gift of God, one after this manner, and another after that.

8 I say therefore to the unmarried and widows, it is good for them if they abide even as I.

9 But if they cannot contain, let them marry: for it is better to marry than to burn.

1 Corinthians 7:10-17   KJV

10 And unto the married I command, yet not I, but the Lord, Let not the wife depart from her husband:

11 But and if she depart, let her remain unmarried or be reconciled to her husband: and let not the husband put away his wife.

12 But to the rest speak I, not the Lord: If any

brother hath a wife that believeth not, and she be pleased to dwell with him, let him not put her away.

13 And the woman which hath an husband that believeth not, and if he be pleased to dwell with her, let her not leave him.

14 For the unbelieving husband is sanctified by the wife, and the unbelieving wife is sanctified by the husband: else were your children unclean; but now are they holy.

15 But if the unbelieving depart, let him depart. A brother or a sister is not under bondage in such cases: but God hath called us to peace.

16 For what knowest thou, O wife, whether thou shalt save thy husband? or how knowest thou, O man, whether thou shalt save thy wife?

17 But as God hath distributed to every man, as the Lord hath called every one, so let him walk. And so ordain I in all churches.

A Commentary on Part 6 Sexual Relations

As you will see in part 7 improper sexual relations is the only justification that Jesus gives authority for a scriptual divorce.

Therefore sexual relations should be a high priority in your marriage.

Your wife burning the toast, or your husband not cutting the grass should not be reasons you allow to prevent this part of your marriage.

God is a big picture God. While we tend to focus on the result God focuses on what lead to the result as well.

John 8:3-11

3 And the scribes and Pharisees brought unto him a woman taken in adultery; and when they had set her in the midst,

4 They say unto him, Master, this woman was taken in adultery, in the very act.

5 Now Moses in the law commanded us, that such should be stoned: but what sayest thou?

6 This they said, tempting him, that they might have to accuse him. But Jesus stooped down, and with his finger wrote on the ground, as though he heard them not.

7 So when they continued asking him, he lifted up himself, and said unto them, He that is without sin among you, let him first cast a stone at her.

8 And again he stooped down, and wrote on the ground.

9 And they which heard it, being convicted by their own conscience, went out one by one, beginning at the eldest, even unto the last: and Jesus was left alone, and the woman standing in the midst.

10 When Jesus had lifted up himself, and saw none but the woman, he said unto her, Woman, where are those thine accusers? hath no man condemned thee?

11 She said, No man, Lord. And Jesus said unto her, Neither do

I condemn thee: go, and sin no more.

From verse 6 we understand that Jesus is aware of the Pharisees motive as well as the act of adultery itself. In verse 11 Jesus shows mercy and gives corrective instruction. Jesus made a judgement based on more than just the act of adultery. He looked at a bigger picture.

Many of us will not feel well, yet we get up, drive to work, work for 8 hours and drive home. All for a boss you may or may not care little about. But find it hard to give 30 minutes of intimacy with our spouse.

1 Corintians 7:5 Defraud ye not one the other, except it be with consent for a time, that ye may give yourselves to fasting and prayer; and come together again, that Satan tempt you not for your incontinency.

The bible meaning of the word incontinency is:

"failure to restrain the passions or appetites; indulgence of lust; lewdness."

Compassion may require a "rain check". But be careful not to allow them to accumulate and allow Satan to tempt you or your spouse.

The gift of celibacy if for before marriage not after...

Divorce is painful expensive and spiritually dangerous. When it comes to sexual relations in your marriage...keep in mind the bigger picture.

PART 7

Marriage Divorce & Remarriage

Luke 16:18　　　KJV

18 Whosoever putteth away his wife, and marrieth another, committeth adultery: and whosoever marrieth her that is put away from her husband committeth adultery.

Matthew 5:32　　　KJV

32 But I say unto you, That whosoever shall put away his wife, saving for the cause of fornication, causeth her to commit adultery: and whosoever shall marry her that is divorced committeth adultery.

Mark 10:6-12　　　KJV

6 But from the beginning of the creation God made them male and female.

7 For this cause shall a man leave his father and mother, and cleave to his wife;

8 And they twain shall be one flesh: so then they are no more twain, but one flesh.

9 What therefore God hath joined together, let not man put asunder.

10 And in the house his disciples asked him again of the same matter.

11 And he saith unto them, Whosoever shall put away his wife, and marry another, committeth adultery against her.

12 And if a woman shall put away her husband, and be married to another, she committeth adultery.

Romans 7:1-3   **KJV**

Know ye not, brethren, (for I speak to them that know the law,) how that the law hath dominion over a man as long as he liveth?

2 For the woman which hath an husband is bound by the law to her husband so long as he liveth; but if the husband be dead, she is loosed from the law of her husband.

3 So then if, while her husband liveth, she be married to another man, she shall be called an adulteress: but if her husband be dead, she is free from that law; so that she is no adulteress, though she be married to another man.

1 Corinthians 7:27-28   **KJV**

27 Art thou bound unto a wife? seek not to be loosed. Art thou loosed from a wife? seek not a wife.

28 But and if thou marry, thou hast not sinned; and if a virgin marry, she hath not sinned. Nevertheless such shall have trouble in the flesh: but I spare you.

Matthew 19:2-12   **KJV**

2 And great multitudes followed him; and he healed them there.

3 The Pharisees also came unto him, tempting him, and saying unto him, Is it lawful for a man to put away his wife for every cause?

4 And he answered and said unto them, Have ye not read, that he which made them at the beginning made them male and female,

5 And said, For this cause shall a man leave father and mother, and shall cleave to his wife: and they twain shall be one flesh?

6 Wherefore they are no more twain, but one flesh. What therefore God hath joined together, let not man put asunder.

7 They say unto him, Why did Moses then command to give a writing of divorcement, and to put her away?

8 He saith unto them, Moses because of the hardness of your hearts suffered you to put away your wives: but from the beginning it was not so.

9 And I say unto you, Whosoever shall put away his wife, except it be for fornication, and shall marry another, committeth adultery: and whoso marrieth her which is put away doth commit adultery.

10 His disciples say unto him, If the case of the man be so with his wife, it is not good to marry.

11 But he said unto them, All men cannot receive this saying, save they to whom it is given.

12 For there are some eunuchs, which were so born from their mother's womb: and there are some eunuchs, which were made eunuchs of men: and there be eunuchs, which have made themselves eunuchs for the kingdom of heaven's sake. He that is able to receive it, let him receive it.

NO MARRIAGE IN HEAVEN

Matthew 22:24-30   KJV

24 Saying, Master, Moses said, If a man die, having no children, his brother shall marry his wife, and raise up seed unto his brother.

25 Now there were with us seven brethren: and the first, when he had married a wife, deceased, and, having no issue, left his wife unto his brother:

26 Likewise the second also, and the third, unto the seventh.

27 And last of all the woman died also.

28 Therefore in the resurrection whose wife shall she be of the seven? for they all had her.

29 Jesus answered and said unto them, Ye do err, not knowing the scriptures, nor the power of God.

30 For in the resurrection they neither marry, nor are given in marriage, but are as the angels of God in heaven.

Frequently Asked Questions about Marriage Divorce and Remarriage

1. What is a Scriptual Divorce?

A scriptual divorce is a divorce based on what the New Testament Scriptures say about divorce.

2. Why the New Testament?

That is the Testament Christians are bound to today Hebrews 9:14-17.

3. What authority does the New Testament give for a scriptural divorce?

Death of the spouse: Romans 7:1-3

Fornication: Matthew 19:9

4. What if I do everything right and my spouse leaves me?

Remain unmarried: 1 Corinthians 7:11

Be Reconciled: 1 Corinthians 7:11

Remarry: Matthew 19:9

If you are offering restoration to the marriage and have not committed fornication and your spouse remarries or commits fornication then according to Matthew 19:9 you would be permitted to remarry.

5. What if I have an abusive or dangerous spouse?

You would have grounds for a legal separation: 1 Corinthians 7:11 & 1 Corinthians 11:15

Then the same scenario described in question 4 would apply.

Remain unmarried, be reconciled or remarry if the spouse has commited fornication during the separation.

6. These rules seem too strict to me.

Marriage is not for everybody: Matthew 19:12

However it is clear that Jesus was well aware of the challenges that can arise in a marriage and made it clear there are eunuchs for the "kingdom of heaven's sake".

That is why Paul said "I would that all men were even as I myself." Single! Single life is not superior to married life(**Ecclesiastes 4:9-12**), however Paul was talking in the context of the safest path for people who were having challenges when it came to sexual relations and putting God's law first.

7. But my Pastor says...

Keep in mind in Matthew 19:7 the followers of Jesus brought Moses into the conversation. Jesus made it clear, there is no other with more authority than Him on the matter. In the end you will have to study for yourself and draw your own conclusions.

The main purpose for this book...

The primary purpose for writing this book and posting it on book sites all over the world, as well as creating a audio book version, was to give the world a basic foundation of the biblical information on the topic of marriage.

Today Our movies, media and television programs are leading people to believe that marriage is just another form of dating. The scriptures state over and over again that marriage is meant to be for life. Therefore it is extremely important that we select the correct partner, based on the word of God.

Reciprocity: the practice of exchanging things with others for mutual benefit, especially privileges granted by one country or organization to another.

If you have selected a like minded person, and treat them as the bible instructs you to do, then reciprocity will likely increase the chances that you have a marriage for life.

Conclusion

The Whole Armour of God

Ephesians 6:11-17

11 Put on the whole armour of God, that ye may be able to stand against the wiles of the devil.

12 For we wrestle not against flesh and blood, but against principalities, against powers, against the rulers of the darkness of this world, against spiritual wickedness in high places.

13 Wherefore take unto you the whole armour of God, that ye may be able to withstand in the evil day, and having done all, to stand.

14 Stand therefore, having your loins girt about with truth, and having on the breastplate of righteousness;

15 And your feet shod with the preparation of the gospel of peace;

16 Above all, taking the shield of faith, wherewith ye shall be able to quench all the fiery darts of the wicked.

17 And take the helmet of salvation, and the sword of the Spirit, which is the word of God:

As you can see from the above scriptures your enemy is not flesh and blood but spiritual. The only offensive weapon you are given is the word of God.

These scriptures are just the beginning of understanding.

There are many bible translations but a study has shown the Kings James Version to be the most accurate to know original text.

Also Understand that Jesus sometimes spoke in

hy·per·bo·le hyperbole; exaggerated statements or claims not meant to be taken literally.

Matthew 5:30 And if thy right hand offend thee, cut it off, and cast it from thee: for it is profitable for thee that one of thy members should perish, and not that thy whole body should be cast into hell.

This scripture Is a good example. That is why I suggest you download a Interlinear Bible so you can view the scriptures in the original greek and Hebrew with the literal english translations. This will deepen your understanding of the true meaning of the scriptures as opposed to another persons interpretation.

To find one, just go to Google and type in: Interlinear Bible

The church needs to do a better job when it comes to our marriages.

Stand on the foundations God has given us in His word and you and your family can have a happy and fruitful life together!

Philippians 4:13 I can do all things through Christ which strengtheneth me.

Disclaimer Notice

This book was written as a guide and for information, educational and entertainment purposes only. No warranties of any kind are expressed or implied.

Readers acknowledge that the author is not engaging in the rendering of legal, financial, medical or professional advice, and the information in this book is not meant to take the place of any professional advice. If advice is needed in any of these fields, you are advised to seek the services of a professional.

While the author has attempted to make the information in this book as accurate as possible, no guarantee is given as to the accuracy or currency of any individual item. Laws and procedures related to business, health and well being are constantly changing.

Therefore, in no event shall the author of this book be liable for any special, indirect, or consequential damages or any damages whatsoever in connection with the use of the information herein provided.

All Rights Reserved

No part of this book may be used or reproduced in any manner whatsoever without the written permission of the author.

Finally, if you enjoyed this book, please take the time to share your thoughts and post a review on Amazon. It'd be greatly appreciated!

Many Thanks,

Brian Mahoney

We want to thank you for the purchase of this book and more importantly, thank you for reading it to the end. We hope your reading experience was pleasurable and that you would inform your family and friends on Facebook, Twitter or other social media.

We would like to continue to provide you with high-quality books, and that end, would you mind leaving us a review on Amazon.com?

Just use the link below, scroll down about 3/4 of the page and you will see images similar to the one below.

We are extremely grateful for your assistance.
Warm Regards, MahoneyProducts Publishing

Book Link:
https://www.amazon.com/dp/B09L3NNZRR

Customer reviews
4.6 out of 5 stars   4.6 out of 5
6 global ratings

5 star   64%
4 star   36%-
3 star 0% (0%)   0%
2 star 0% (0%)   0%
1 star 0% (0%)

Review this product
Share your thoughts with other customers
(Write a Customer Review)

You might also enjoy:

Just Use the Book Link Below:

https://www.amazon.com/dp/1974314634

2 Timothy 2:15 (KJV)Study to shew thyself approved unto God, a workman that needeth not to be ashamed, rightly dividing the word of truth.

Before Paul met Jesus, he was sincere, but sincerely wrong. If the truth can be rightly divided it can be wrongly divided.

Discover....

* Bible Verses that teach us how to accurately understand the Bible and rightly divide the truth.

* Who wrote the Bible? If you can not show a person that the Bible is the Word of God, then all of the other scriptures will be of no use. All's it takes is a little "wedge of doubt" to cost a person their salvation.

* Bible Verses that prove by Science, Prophesy, and by eye witness, who wrote the Bible and why it is, without a doubt the word of God.

Discover what the Bibles says God's scriptural plan of salvation is...

not what many TV preachers/entertainers say...

"Not every one that saith unto me, Lord, Lord, shall enter into the kingdom of heaven;" Matthew 7:21

"Howbeit in vain do they worship me, teaching for doctrines the commandments of men." Mark 7:7

Even people who consider Jesus their Lord will be denied entrance into the Kingdom of Heaven.

Don't be one of them! Don't wait...today is the day of salvation tomorrow may be to late...

www.ingramcontent.com/pod-product-compliance
Lightning Source LLC
Chambersburg PA
CBHW052120110526
44592CB00013B/1692

THE WISEST COUNSELOR TO A CHRISTIAN MARRIAGE IS GOD!

MATTHEW 7:24 THEREFORE WHOSOEVER HEARETH THESE SAYINGS OF MINE, AND DOETH THEM, I WILL LIKEN HIM UNTO A WISE MAN, WHICH BUILT HIS HOUSE UPON A ROCK: 25 AND THE RAIN DESCENDED, AND THE FLOODS CAME, AND THE WINDS BLEW, AND BEAT UPON THAT HOUSE; AND IT FELL NOT: FOR IT WAS FOUNDED UPON A ROCK.

CHRISTIAN MARRIAGE COUNSELING BOOK OF BIBLE VERSES
MARRIAGE SCRIPTURES TO HELP WOMEN, MEN, KIDS, MOMS & COUPLES WITH INTIMACY, SEX & COMMUNICATION
BY BRIAN MAHONEY

DISCOVER...

INTRODUCTION: RIGHTLY DIVIDING THE TRUTH
PART 1: SCRIPTURES FOR SELECTING A PARTNER
PART 2: SCRIPTURES ON THE BENEFITS OF MARRIAGE
PART 3: SCRIPTURES ON LOVE RESPECT & FORGIVE ONE ANOTHER
PART 4: SCRIPTURES WITH INSTRUCTIONS FOR MEN
PART 5: SCRIPTURES WITH INSTRUCTIONS FOR WOMEN
PART 6: SCRIPTURES ON SEXUAL RELATIONS
PART 7: SCRIPTURES ON MARRIAGE, DIVORCE & REMARRIAGE
CONCLUSION: THE WHOLE ARMOUR OF GOD

DIVORCE IS EXPENSIVE AND CAN LEAD TO A LIFETIME OF PAIN. MARRIAGE IS TO IMPORTANT TO GET IT WRONG!
WHETHER YOU ARE JUST STARTING OUT, OR SEEKING RESTORATION TO YOUR MARRIAGE, KNOW EXACTLY WHAT GOD'S ADVICE IS FOR YOUR MARRIAGE.

2 TIMOTHY 3:15 AND THAT FROM A CHILD THOU HAST KNOWN THE HOLY SCRIPTURES, WHICH ARE ABLE TO MAKE THEE WISE UNTO SALVATION THROUGH FAITH WHICH IS IN CHRIST JESUS. 16 ALL SCRIPTURE IS GIVEN BY INSPIRATION OF GOD, AND IS PROFITABLE FOR DOCTRINE, FOR REPROOF, FOR CORRECTION, FOR INSTRUCTION IN RIGHTEOUSNESS: 17 THAT THE MAN OF GOD MAY BE PERFECT, THOROUGHLY FURNISHED UNTO ALL GOOD WORKS

STEPHEN FOFANOFF

YOU'RE
WHAT JESUS REALLY SAID
NOT
AND WHY IT MATTERS
BROKEN